Good
Character
Traits

Humility

Ashley Lee

Explore other books at:
WWW.ENGAGEBOOKS.COM

VANCOUVER, B.C.

WWW.ENGAGEBOOKS.COM

Humility: Good Character Traits
Lee, Ashley, 1995 –
Text © 2025 Engage Books
Design © 2025 Engage Books

Edited by: A.R. Roumanis
Design by: Mandy Christiansen

Text set in Myriad Pro Regular.
Chapter headings set in Anton.

FIRST EDITION / FIRST PRINTING

LIBRARY AND ARCHIVES CANADA CATALOGUING IN PUBLICATION

Title: Humility / Ashley Lee.
Names: Lee, Ashley, author.
Description: Series statement: Good Character Traits

ISBN 978-1-77878-738-6 (hardcover)
ISBN 978-1-77878-744-7 (softcover)

This project has been made possible in part
by the Government of Canada.

Canada

Humility

Contents

What Is Humility?

Humility is when someone knows what they are and are not good at. They know that they do not know everything.

Humility does not mean you do not like yourself.

People who are **humble** do not think they are better than other people. They know that someone else might be better at something.

Key Word

Humble: have humility.

Why Is Humility Important?

People who are not humble cannot always see when they make a mistake. This stops them from learning from their mistakes.

Humility helps people see their mistakes and learn from them. It allows people to grow and change.

What Does Humility Look Like?

People who are humble think about what other people are thinking or feeling. They are good at listening to other people.

People who are humble are not afraid of making mistakes. They do not show off or **brag** about the things they are good at.

Key Word

Brag: when someone talks a lot about how great they are at something.

How Does Humility Affect You?

Humility helps you get better at things. You cannot get better at something if you think you know everything.

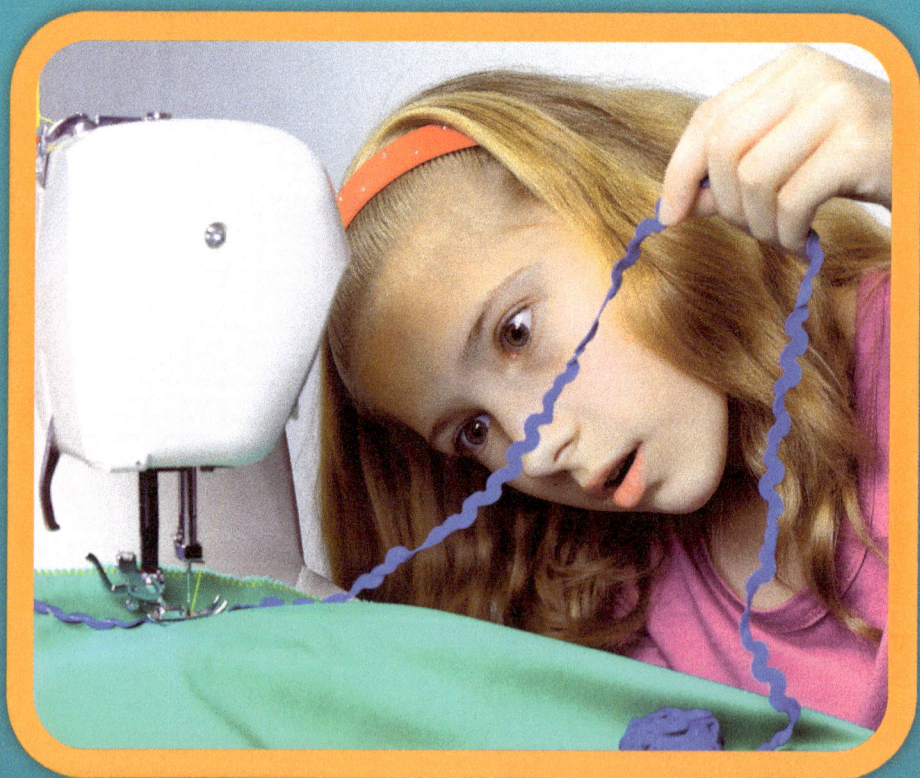

Understanding that you do not know everything makes you **curious**. You want to know more so you ask lots of questions.

Key Word

Curious: want to know more about something.

How Does Humility Affect Others?

Humility helps people spread kindness. Telling a friend that they did a good job in class helps them feel good about themselves.

People who are humble like to help other people. They think less about themselves and more about the people around them.

Is Everyone Humble?

Not everyone is humble. Some people want to be the best at everything or think they are better than others.

Other people think they are not good at anything. They might put themselves down a lot or say they do not like themselves.

Talk to a trusted adult if you have a hard time seeing good things about yourself.

Is It Bad if You Are Not Humble?

People who are not humble can sometimes be mean to other people. Sometimes they are mean to themselves.

It is okay to forget to be humble sometimes. Nobody is perfect. But it is important to say sorry if you made someone feel bad.

Does Humility Change Over Time?

People can become more or less humble as they get older. **Practicing** humility can make someone more humble.

Key Word

Practicing: doing something over and over again to get better at it.

Some people feel a lot of **pressure** from other people to be the best at everything. This can make them less humble over time.

Key Word

Pressure: when someone tries to get someone else to do something.

Is It Hard to Be Humble?

It can be hard to be humble when you want to be the best. But it is okay to be good at something without being the best.

It can also be hard to be humble without putting yourself down. Many people have a hard time with this.

How Can You Learn to Be More Humble?

Think about how other people might be feeling. You might make a friend feel bad if you brag about winning a game they lost.

It is okay to be upset if you make a mistake. But try not to let one mistake make your whole day bad.

Practicing humility can make it easier to be okay with making mistakes.

How Can You Help Others Be More Humble?

Do not just tell others about humility. Be a good **example** to them. Show them what humility looks like.

Key Word

Example: a way to show something to help someone understand.

Let other people know it is okay to make mistakes. Do not make fun of someone for the mistakes they make.

How to Be Humble Every Day

1. Listen when other people talk.

2. Say sorry if you make a mistake.

Key Word

Compliment: kind words that show someone you like what they have done.

3. Compliment other people.

4. Ask for help when you need it.

27

Humility Around the World

Different **cultures** around the world have different art styles. Each kind of art tells a story about that culture.

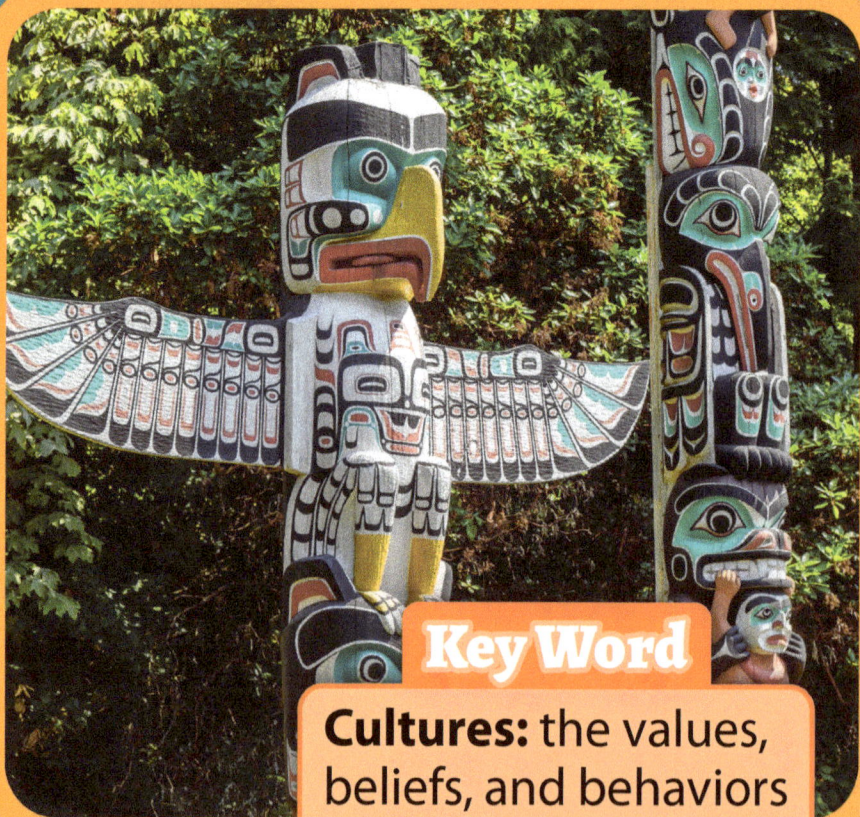

Key Word

Cultures: the values, beliefs, and behaviors of a group of people.

People do not think their art style is better than everyone else's. They are humble and know that all art styles are important.

Quiz

Test your knowledge of humility by answering the following questions. The questions are based on what you have read in this book. The answers are listed on the bottom of the next page.

1 Does humility mean you do not like yourself?

2 What does humility help people see?

3 What does humility help people spread?

4 Is it okay to forget to be humble sometimes?

5 Is it okay to be good at something without being the best?

6 What should you do when other people talk?

Explore Other Level 2 Readers.

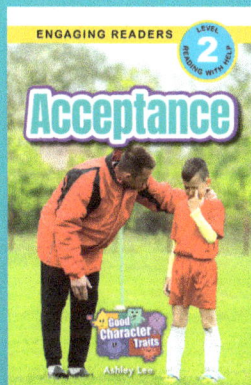

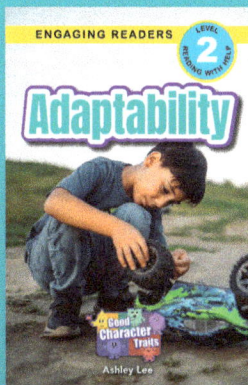

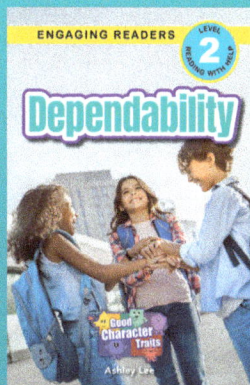

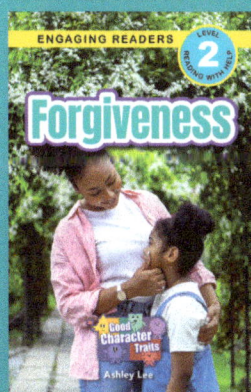

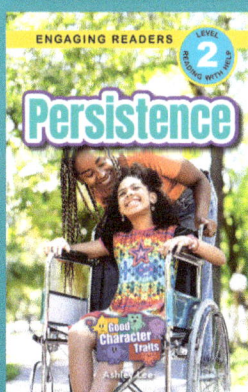

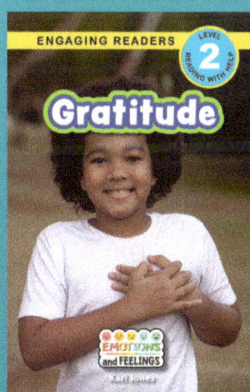

ENGAGING READERS — LEVEL 2 READING WITH HELP

Acceptance
Good Character Traits
Ashley Lee

Adaptability
Good Character Traits
Ashley Lee

Dependability
Good Character Traits
Ashley Lee

Forgiveness
Good Character Traits
Ashley Lee

Persistence
Good Character Traits
Ashley Lee

Gratitude
EMOTIONS and FEELINGS
Karl Jones

Grief
EMOTIONS and FEELINGS
Sarah Harvey

Love
EMOTIONS and FEELINGS
Sarah Harvey

Worry
EMOTIONS and FEELINGS
Sarah Harvey

Visit www.engagebooks.com/readers

www.ingramcontent.com/pod-product-compliance
Lightning Source LLC
Chambersburg PA
CBHW052035030426
42337CB00027B/5021